KIND PRAISE FOR *THE MOONFLOWER MONOLOGUES*

"There is something wistful and necessary about this collection of poetry by Tess Guinery. With *The Moonflower Monologues* Tess moves from the warm summertime insinuations of her previous works to perceiving the embrace of night as an intimate opportunity. She returns to crafting language that is hopeful and introspective, while cupping her reflections like water held in two deft and careful hands. The strength and femininity offered in these poems is kind, still and honest. Just as she says in one piece, 'Begin, again.' These poems are not just blooming conceptions; they are art that inspires one to find breath where breath may have been lacking. This is a most welcome addition to the world of art and language gathering around women today."

—Teresa Archer, *Darling* magazine

"*The Moonflower Monologues* offer deep and profound insights on hope and creativity. Tess Guinery has a unique expression of love that uses the poetic form to dive into the human senses with clear intention and purity. This collection is bursting with life and passion and eagerly invites the reader to wander off into their most wildest of dreams."

—Tess Roy, creative director, Mosaic

"I love how in Tess's enchanting prose, the focus is always on illuminating, healing, brightening, and freeing the parts of the soul that are kept in the shadows of captivity. She challenges conventional wisdom in ways that are delicate even as they are fierce. Her words always lend me courage and leave my heart brimming with love and moondust."

—Skie Peterson, writer

THE
MOONFLOWER
MONOLOGUES

Tess Guinery

Andrews McMeel
PUBLISHING®

Andrews McMeel Publishing
a division of Andrews McMeel Universal
1130 Walnut Street, Kansas City, Missouri 64106

www.andrewsmcmeel.com

21 22 23 24 25 SDB 10 9 8 7 6 5 4 3 2 1

ISBN: 978-1-5248-6750-8

Library of Congress Control Number:
2021903894

Editor: Kevin Kotur
Cover Art and Creative Direction: Tess Guinery
Designer: Tiffany Meairs
Production Editor: Dave Shaw
Production Manager: Carol Coe
Talent Management: Holly Masters

The Moonflower Monologues was originally self-published in 2019 by Morgan Printing, Sydney, Australia, thanks to the management of Holly Masters, the mentorship of Skie Peterson, and editing from Melissa Thielmann.

ATTENTION: SCHOOLS AND BUSINESSES:
Andrews McMeel books are available at quantity discounts with bulk purchase for educational, business, or sales promotional use. For information, please e-mail the Andrews McMeel Publishing Special Sales Department: specialsales@amuniversal.com.

Dedicated to the bloomers.

Midnight igniters, nighttime revolutionaries, moonlit encouragers, catalysts for growth: the crowns of those who bravely stand and bloom in the shadows of the moon—leaning in and leaning up, heart-shaped hands and fragrant notes from life songs pointing out promises in the violet canopies above—and all, just to herald the coming dawn for another and watch them grow victoriously taller, blooming into their new day—

The Moonflower.

She was written in the shadows,
beneath the blankets of silent nights.

Her words—violet milk.
Her pages—golden tissues for diamond tears.

The perfumes of her pages fly high,
settling on beds of flowers.
Light—sewn into her every syllable,
holding anthems that carry hearts over bitter seas.

She is a scented, dancing whisper,
eyes closed, riding the wind,
her paper hands seeking wisdom's gift,
while trekking naked and thin-skinned—

So, just as a moonflower
dares to stand and bloom,
growing bright and free,
in the shadows of the moon;

May these gentle pages,
when planted just like seeds,
carry breath to move you (& others)
through the valleys and messy seas—

In the shadows—blooming.

Are you in the deep, fumbling for the light? Adhere, sweet friend, there's much to be found (in the hidden places).

Are your eyes facing north, the change written brightly on the sun? Run into the rays.

Is your heart hungry for truth & flowers? Eat such things for breakfast.

Wherever you are standing—stand.

Words come when they do. These monologues were written standing in the dark; their words flow in order of their sojourn in corners of my mind. And some were tucked in unexpectedly when the sounds fell upon cold valley floors— an imperfectly arranged soliloquy. Delve into their accidental choruses that bring moments to fall and moments to rise. Chew them slowly (savoring some for later) and for those with hours ahead— begin at the dawning and close beneath the midnight canopy, in one, slow, sitting.

Lean into the pages, but only if you hold a violet milk in one hand or honeyed rum in the other.

THE
MOONFLOWER
MONOLOGUES

The stars nodded,
The ocean agreed,
The flowers chorused,
"Bloom now—bloom free"

Rise, again.

THE
MOONFLOWER
MONOLOGUES

These words, they were found in the shadows, in the half-light silence, on the early summer mornings, during the "come up for air" walks alone, underneath puddles of tears, and through round-and-round-the-bend kind of conversations that went on way too late into the night, communion with friends and family and him, glasses overflowing, while I begged my eyes to stay open.

Sometimes words are in the wind,
other times,
buried under rocks.

Both require different means of discovery:
one requires stillness,
and the other—
adventure.

Love in essence:
enfolding as unrefined gold.
In application:
fluid as water between opals.

Sometimes it looks like a chase,
other times—letting go.
Sometimes it's soft,
other times, slow.

It's a beautiful bunch of flowers,
a behind-the-scenes dance,
prayers in the evening,
timely words, or pure romance.

Love needs no crowns,
neither mentions nor accolades.
And most of the time, you'll find
that love—

Love is brave.

THE
MOONFLOWER
MONOLOGUES

Words don't come cheap or easy—nor without quiet treks through shadowed terrain; they are usually found in the residue of midnight tears and morning mulls over remedial caffeine.

I'm learning that every mountaintop revelation requires a long, steep walk. A walk where summits are invitations for glorious reflections and brave shouts of testimony—honoring all that has been. Be sure to stop, drink, and make an occasion of it—with your words, your stories, the clinking of vessels, and songs. Breathe in the clean, loving air, and exhale—large and long. Gather all your creative fire and let light burn in your hands.

In moments like these, one can't camp for long. With eyes looking ahead, from the very mountaintop on which we stand to the valley floor, alluding to the next capstone—

THE
MOONFLOWER
MONOLOGUES

Go on an adventure and discover *whose* you are. This adventure aches for your courage, found deep in the daring places, calling us home—

Maybe when you find whose you are, it's here you'll find who you are.

THE
MOONFLOWER
MONOLOGUES

It was just a tiny seed—
but with a little water
and a little sun,
who knew?
An orchard of apricots!
A place we rested,
dappled in light,
catching our breath
for a little while—

THE
MOONFLOWER
MONOLOGUES

Covered in milk at midnight, words
falling over the edge of the couch
and making puddles on the lounge
room floor—spilling out again, a
recognizable and familiar rumble—
loud sounds warring and bumping
heads with one another. It was as
though each word was fighting for
its chance at a sentence, and as the
tension built, the words blazed into
a zillion flower petals, taking ground
on the messy floor of my heart—my
hands dared to scoop them up, using
them as tissues to wipe away tears
and milk stains, all in the shadows
(and light) of the moon.

THE MOONFLOWER
MONOLOGUES

The true heartbeat behind
anything and everything
is always revealed . . .
eventually—

An invitation to let wrongs go.

THE
MOONFLOWER
MONOLOGUES

Ever prayed an honest prayer?
The bold kind,
nonchalant about its answer
but fearless nonetheless?

I did one eve.
And as the sun rose the very next day,
swift and grand,
an answer came, the most beautiful kind:
no credit to the labor of my hands,
the only lifting: my palms upturned to pray.

Lavish prayers don't necessarily ensure
lofty answers.
Sit with your honest heart
and speak it simply,
nonchalant about its answer,
fearless nonetheless.

THE
MOONFLOWER
MONOLOGUES

Speak to the shadows,
sing into the blue,
dare to speak in color,
a heart will soar (and bloom)—

Rising, above.

THE
MOONFLOWER
MONOLOGUES

As the smoky scent of sage leaves
filled her room, she took rest
among her collection of scattered
quartz and paper promises.

And there she wondered: could
it be that placing her entire
existence into one name was way
too simple a gift to receive?

If you ever find your journey
supposed by another,
take it as a nudge (to choose)
to assume the best in others—

Soften.

THE
MOONFLOWER
MONOLOGUES

Every. Single. Human.

Is on a . . .

J o   u   r n e y.

THE
MOONFLOWER
MONOLOGUES

Sometimes, space is required to do
the things that must be done deep
in the soils of the heart, alone—

Fields.

Gratitude in her bones;
improvisation in her pockets.

Find yourself a floral dress;
her cotton—silver,
her lining—honey silk.

Pick her up off the bedroom floor,
and dare to begin—

Drape her Summer across your
day-glow shoulders, and maybe
your heart will catch up—

Begin, again.

May the battles in your bones
be the lucent to your growth;
may the stretching of your heart
bloom to brightly colored art—

Prelude to a radical victory.

THE
MOONFLOWER
MONOLOGUES

That day.
That foggy,
somber day—
I woke, asleep.

Heavy hues of gray
blanketing vision
(and heart).

My tongue—thick and dry.
My toes—dragging the sand in circles.

I knew it then
as I know it now:
songs lift me out.

So, I sang to my heart,
It is well, it is well—
all the help I needed
to remember what I had forgotten.

All things work together for good . . .
and good they become furthermore—

Declare.

THE
MOONFLOWER
MONOLOGUES

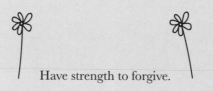

Have strength to forgive.

THE
MOONFLOWER
MONOLOGUES

Surrendering justice:
leaving the details to God.

With one last glimpse earthward,
the valley of all that has been, I fix
my gaze on the summits ahead and
know a work is being done in me.

I'll dare to trek,
and I'll dare to sing—
even if it's loud.

You've changed everything for me.

So I'll never stop telling of your
beauty—

Vow.

THE
MOONFLOWER
MONOLOGUES

Wayfarer,
Word-bearer,
Troubadour—
Evermore.

I packaged up my hopeful hopes
and left a trail of paper notes.
The mountain was big;
I felt human & small,
though I was never alone:
you were there
through it all—

Odyssey.

THE
MOONFLOWER
MONOLOGUES

When you give a gift,
wrap it with French paper,
wild honeysuckles,
and handwritten poems—
but without string.

THE
MOONFLOWER
MONOLOGUES

I have learned that no man can heal my
infirmity, nor bind my gaping wounds.
The elixir: spirit & soil, truth & love.
The Great Physician: Heart Maker,
Heart Keeper, love, unrelenting—
unfailing—undying . . . for You.

THE
MOONFLOWER
MONOLOGUES

Epiphanies under the blue canopy—

Twilight revolutionaries.

Surrender, you sweet and sunny song. You take my handfuls of breath—and make art with all my unknowns.

Favor isn't a mystical force, flying you out and above your worried woes, saving you from cold valley floors.

Favor is a shield, hemming you in, behind and before—calling you out, gifting you with eyes to see, opening your heart to receive the treasures found on narrow paths and even under stones.

THE
MOONFLOWER
MONOLOGUES

The gracious and unoffendable have likely
been pressed the most: they bloom and rise,
out and above, again and again—again.

When we are attached to the vine,
we no longer
need.

In the sunset of my now, I fix my
gaze on the sunrise to come—

Accord.

I'll try better tomorrow—

Motherhood.

They say there's no such thing as "the one"
but there is only one you.

THE
MOONFLOWER
MONOLOGUES

Anything you see to be beautiful:

Is.
His.
Heart.

And suddenly—
the dreams started chasing me.

If I choose to grow,
maybe they will sprout
like a wildflower—

A mother's irresistible invitation.

THE
MOONFLOWER
MONOLOGUES

Let your vulnerability fall into the light,
and they will know it's not a place they'd
fear to tread—

A mother's irresistible invitation, again.

THE
MOONFLOWER
MONOLOGUES

Even in the chaos, don't forget to kiss.

THE
MOONFLOWER
MONOLOGUES

Let time go & watch it grow—

It's an upside-down kingdom.

THE
MOONFLOWER
MONOLOGUES

Prose has become much like a fluid,
full stop for me, a beautifully kind little
dot placed at the end of a thousand
thoughts that finally form into a midnight
epiphany. Something in me always knows
that eventually the words will arrive at
hope—I'll never stop believing that, ever.

Never in my life have I felt so happy & so exhausted, so "into it" & so "over it," so beautiful & so worse for wear, so alive & so tired, so organized & so unorganized, so on the front foot & so on the back foot, so hopeful & so unsure, so visionary & so withdrawn, so extroverted & so introverted, so brave & so afraid, so bold & so timid, so in love & so out of my depth, so abundant & so fickle, so confident & so crazy, so purposeful & so aimless, so intentional & so "go with the flow"—

Motherhood.

PS: Today I need the coffee.

THE
MOONFLOWER
MONOLOGUES

If love is all you need—then we have it all.

Kiss her on the brow,
tell her she's a star,
send her for a shower
and scenic drives in the car.

Make her cups of tea,
sway with her by night
when babes are fast asleep,
with music on, by candlelight.

Pray throughout the day,
look at her with love,
kiss beneath the morning light,
sing to the heavens above—

How he loves (me).

THE MOONFLOWER
MONOLOGUES

I have three daughters.
One of the prettiest sentences
I ever did speak.

The sound of the car wheels pulling
up in the driveway: one of the best
sounds I have ever heard—

Him, coming home.

Those who reveal the wanderings
of others, wearing it like a garland
of floral, reveal something unfloral
of themselves.

THE
MOONFLOWER
MONOLOGUES

"Can you see that purple peak,
adorned with silver sunflowers
cascading from the top?"

THE
MOONFLOWER
MONOLOGUES

Sometimes, a stream of consciousness is best streamed upward, rather than outward. Sometimes it's prayer that should be our safe place to share.

Not all thoughts need to fall upon the ears (and shoulders) of another.

Mull, wrestle, seek in the hidden places, where grace covers all brokenness and the arrows of unhealed thoughts can fly about, without poking eyes out along the way.

Dare to let wisdom shape the arrows into daisies so that the undertone of our sounds may be girded with heaven.

And it's here we can face the hardest of conflicts—sometimes without speaking a single word, large or small.

I'm painting paintings but I want this to be more than painting paintings. I'm writing writings but I want this to be more than writing writings—

I speak of the moon (much):
how she glows,
her phases,
her beauty,
the way she lights up the darkness,
her talent for reflection.

She's a night-chaser,
heart-racer,
moving the ocean tides,
sending me half-crescent smiles,
enticing my waning heart to rise.

But it's not her who takes my breath away;
it's the hands that fashioned her so. I like to
think that she was placed there just for me,
all so she would reflect something tangible
about my maker. . . .

That maybe, He's a wild romantic—
And this is why I love the moon (most).

The things that are sewn in the shadows
of the moon are different from what grows
amid the celebratory festoons—

Both, equally important.

THE
MOONFLOWER
MONOLOGUES

The world of the generous is large.

Anything can be made from
something, and something can be
made from nothing—

Improvisers.

THE
MOONFLOWER
MONOLOGUES

New wine—new ground.
New song—new sound.

Sometimes, it's only God who can see the full intricacies of our complications—

When prayer remedies.

May your yes be yes
and your no be no,
from the ends of your braids,
to the tips of your toes—

Nobility.

THE
MOONFLOWER
MONOLOGUES

Take notice of what light does—to everything.

I'm learning there are some things
that can't be taught in the space
of shortcuts, but rather must be
cultivated on the frontlines—
the long way, knee-deep in
mud, fumbling in the dark, or
in the mess and when you are
daring to be beautifully—brave.

THE
MOONFLOWER
MONOLOGUES

Promises made in haste
are promises best left to waste.

THE MOONFLOWER
MONOLOGUES

We crave stillness; we create.
We create; we crave stillness.
We crave stillness; we create.
We create; we crave stillness—

The process.

In chaos, I choose stillness;
in the grit, my breath finds grace.
In the moment, my skin knows spirit;
in my weariness, my heart finds space.

In the solace, I'll immerse myself,
so in the rolling routines, I can sway.
In the mess, I'll pray till dawn light,
so in the anxious waiting, I lay.

And when my pillow holds my head,
I'll dream, again—

A self-talk paradox walk.

THE
MOONFLOWER
MONOLOGUES

Sipping with the wise,
hungry for what's true,
warring through the storms,
side by side (with you)—

Togetherness.

Those who choose to understand where you have been are the ones who are able to celebrate the colors of your victories—most.

I want to learn where people have been—more.

THE
MOONFLOWER
MONOLOGUES

One soul sharing with another:
a ribbon threading through to eternity,
from the beginning of time until its end,
passing on recipes for life—
their love,
their gifts of faith,
healing and kindness;
generation to generation—

A thread of gold love,
where knots dare not gather,
where silk eternally pours—

New wine, going further.

Get out the ink and paper; write commas and full stops later—

Dance.

Your pearls are for the precious—the
heart nurturers and nourishers, not
for just anyone—

Know the places where you can rest
your head (and heart).

Live your dreams and we will live
them with you—

Friendship.

Intuition: one of God's many voices.

I know a voice that rides on the winds—
it sounds like a whisper
powerful enough to silence hurricanes.

Side by side,
shaping,
defining,
releasing,

lifting us over
impossible things;
our vibrations ascending to heights our
hearts couldn't fathom before—

Dancing.

THE
MOONFLOWER
MONOLOGUES

Holding one's parlance: subtle magnificence.

A lantern in one hand,
a bright, fierce heart in the other—
one willing to face the storm
coming ferociously for you (with you).

She elevates,
celebrates,
upholds, and protects.
She is one willing
to humbly curl into your most harrowing corners
with nothing but a garland of grace—

Friendship.

THE
MOONFLOWER
MONOLOGUES

Words are velvet, tactile sounds.

Front-footedly on the back foot—

Motherhood.

THE MOONFLOWER
MONOLOGUES

Your voice was loud
in the crowd,
my girl,
your voice was loud
in the crowd—

Lanterns.

Acquire good taste within conversation, and you'll acquire less tolerance for anything less.

Wisdom had breath before mountains were sculpted, before horizons were known to have no end, before diamond-shaped ornaments were hung across grand, velvet expanses—all by hand.

Her whispers—applauding the beginnings of creation, while her songs wrapped themselves around every color with whole-hearted affirmations.

Her scents—spilling out like paint upon every make of movement.
Her words—sewing stories into every stone and flower.

She is a mystery—a truthful, honest mystery—encouraging the most beautiful kind of curiosity, leading not to the ends of nothing but to the beginnings of
E V E R Y T H I N G !

And if you ever make the time to turn the stones she gifts, it's home you'll find for your sweet and messy soul.

Breathe in all the change
as though your lungs depend
on the promise of new beginnings—
reminiscent, embracing ends.

THE
MOONFLOWER
MONOLOGUES

Where you choose to unravel matters.

Leave your explanations down by
the shore, and let the higher tides
wash them away; see them swirl
and twirl, and when they land in
lagoons, may the sounds of dusk
silence their echoes—

Dance.

Her clay heart,
a million pieces
spread over the dusty earth.

She drew a deep breath—
and with all the gold & stars & faith she had,
she crowned herself the thoroughly inexperienced
and put her hope in another.

This—a kind of radical.

THE MOONFLOWER
MONOLOGUES

You lent me your skin
when mine was too thin.
You held me tender.
You loved me brighter.

I'm learning to let some battles be
fought not with swords but with songs,
in quiet places behind closed doors—

Prayer.

THE
MOONFLOWER
MONOLOGUES

May we not try to figure everything out on our own.

THE
MOONFLOWER
MONOLOGUES

Peace arrives on the eve of the right decision
and rises on the sun of the way forward.

THE
MOONFLOWER
MONOLOGUES

When we view those darkened places,
while standing in the light, may we
honor the role of the shadows and
wrap our thankfulness in bouquets—

Perspective.

THE
MOONFLOWER
MONOLOGUES

You thought it was a mask;
in truth it was a shield.

Throw your time into the potpourri of the wind, where your senses need no chains; let time return to its wild fragrances, into the ink of its Author's hand.

Let the one who is above the seasons—the maker of each sunrise—take the seconds of your day . . .

and return them, tenfold*

*mysteriously extended time within limited time.

Sometimes,
willingly,
I'm guilty of golden-age thinking—

Imagineering.

THE
MOONFLOWER
MONOLOGUES

Kindness: intelligence.
Fortitude: wisdom.
Gentleness: self-control.
Empathy: generosity.
Thoughtfulness: selflessness.
Openheartedness: worthiness.
Good talk: soul healthiness.
Tears: tenderness.
Freedom: a recipient of perfect *love*.

A Creator who creates: moonflowers, shooting stars, lavender, ocean tides, blooms, stones, color & butterflies, sunsets of purple, morning mist, dandelions, mangoes, mountains, rivers, fire, valleys, honey & time, light, laughter, coffee beans, planets, grapes, palm trees, fragrances, rhythms, opals, rain, B R E A T H mysteries, fireflies, clouds, jungles, pine trees, sound, dazzling rainbows, giraffes, jellyfish, lightning, wind, sand, gold, humans, dreams, dance, hearts, miracles & LOVE, day & night, night & day—is a Creator I want to follow with my whole, entire heart.

She acknowledged she was limited
& that's when life became limitless.

Even her breakfast was poetry.

I'm learning to be more gracious and to
stand in the shoes of others—humbly.

Purpose is something you can't deny. It will knock on the door of your heart until you are home.

The mirage of January gifts the new year February.

How can one year begin without habitudes of space in between?

Lacuna.

What's sown in silence is important (& sacred).

Some things can't be written in sugar, only salt.

✻

Treasure is hidden in the shadows.

�֍

✻

✻

A heart submitted to the garden of
healing is not dependent on others.

THE
MOONFLOWER
MONOLOGUES

Undress the sounds of your feet—then write.

THE
MOONFLOWER
MONOLOGUES

He'll turn up "Harvest Moon," and I'll know that it's gonna be one of those nights: the nights that are ours, our way, our wild. I love how we do nights, we do them well—it's our thing—leaving the dishes sprawled across our silver benches (even though it irks us equally) because we know that the evening silence is more important to us right now; and, after talking about all the wonderful & impossible things, we lie down to sleep and you whisper, "I love us."

Drifting to other lands as we lie in the dust of harvest moon melodies, we fall asleep.

The songs that are flying high and burning their notes into the ceiling of our home will one day burn the walls of our hearts, affectionately—

Nostalgic perfume.

THE
MOONFLOWER
MONOLOGUES

Shield sound thinking; choose what comes in.

103

Motives soiled in doubles will see you enter twisted troubles.

Dancing & writing—
not dissimilar.
Both are full-bodied
& move.

If you were to break open the words
of my pen, I pray light would pour out
from them—from their bones—light.

And, no matter how dark it was when
they were written, may every syllable
& rhyme bear witness: even in the
shadows, when connected to the
source, *There. Is. Light.*

I'm learning creativity is important and
that painting art at night is sometimes
better than a good night's sleep.

THE
MOONFLOWER
MONOLOGUES

The golden thinker in me,
she was lost (for a while)—
Week in,
week out,
dawn to dark,
head in my palms;
adrift in the hollow places of an unkind
familiar, mean sounds circled and moments
blurred as I let the echoes nestle.

Suddenly (it's always suddenly), an old-time
breeze more fragrant than ever before—
called me back home.

I don't know how the weight lifted so
quickly, after days and days in the mud,
but something tells me it was the voice of
another fighting on my behalf—

& later that day, I learned it to be true—

The prayers of another.

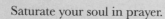

Saturate your soul in prayer.

Write & release,
receive free peace—

Paper prayers.

"I'm doing a new thing."

Setting apart the petals from the water,
the trail blazed with uncertainty,
no point of reference—
just words
pooling in a rose-scented shower—
And my heart knew,
even in my aloneness,
I'd eventually arrive at the unwritten—

Shower prayers.

Are we not peculiar?
A pure oddity?

My lungs: full of clean, cloudless air when
I'm lighting candles alone.

You: shimmering to life in the presence of
company & rowdy conversation—

Penchants.

THE
MOONFLOWER
MONOLOGUES

Gathered in the kindness of women—

Womankind.

Dance with the wise;
stand for what's true.
That way, when the wild things come,
your heart will know what to do.

THE
MOONFLOWER
MONOLOGUES

Beginnings have middles and middles have ends.

All was loud & I went to bed
soundly because heaven was fighting
for me—

Peace (beyond understanding).

THE
MOONFLOWER
MONOLOGUES

Expecting answers from sticks &
stones, rituals & wishbones—

A cul-de-sac endeavor.

God met me in the shower.
Water falling,
both from my eyes and from above.
I asked Him,
"Is it okay that I feel this way?"
And He said, "It is."

And I remember so clearly
crying out the heaviness.
My humanity, not at all new, to Him.

Make time to discover the places where you can best *be*—"in it, but not of it" & "of it, and all about it."

I clean my entire house just so I can
make a mess, again—

The creative process.

THE
MOONFLOWER
MONOLOGUES

May the shadows not hold you;
may they grow you.

May we stop trying to make safe sense of others; let our hearts yearn to throw away the hearsay, acknowledging and appreciating that nothing stays the same— what once was, isn't necessarily what is.

Approach each other with the mercies of a new day.

Find friends who feel more comfy dancing
in the victory of your flowers than wrapped
in the weeds of your pain.

I plan—my Creator enables.

THE
MOONFLOWER
MONOLOGUES

Good paths are narrow, leading to wide and spacious living (in fields of flowers).

What happens behind closed doors—their fight, their sweat, their tears—is a mystery to us all. Unless we are painting stories of hope (across the life of another), maybe don't paint at all.

THE
MOONFLOWER
MONOLOGUES

Largeness of soul,
mind,
heart,
spirit,
conversation,
dreams—

A visionary's outfit.

THE
MOONFLOWER
MONOLOGUES

Wisdom teaches us how to create bounds
with fragrant petals and moveable oceans:
she waters our floral hedges, points out the
rips in the tides, and in love she whispers,
"These will keep your heart safe and keep
your heart pretty."—

Boundaries.

THE
MOONFLOWER
MONOLOGUES

Have yourself some non-negotiables—
then add
contours & light,
water & salt,
and then live—barefoot in flowers.

Wisdom: she shows us how to
do really hard things in really
beautiful ways.

THE
MOONFLOWER
MONOLOGUES

When the soul is known, daily
banter isn't easily misinterpreted—

Friendship.

THE
MOONFLOWER
MONOLOGUES

After months of feeling like a droopy
flower, I prayed: "Who do you say I am?"
A question I knew should only be answered
by One.

THE
MOONFLOWER
MONOLOGUES

The words of others do not define you.

Exfoliate . . . shed . . . feel—

The process.

Wild things happen in stillness.

THE
MOONFLOWER
MONOLOGUES

I won't let you go back down the prickly path from whence you came—

Womankind.

Every so often, sit with your solitude
and see what it says—

Echoes.

I'm learning many things: friendship &
love & purpose & sacredness & culling &
mulling & time. I'm learning about non-
negotiables: heart ratios, my *whys* my
whens & my now—

Unravel.

138

May we not let ourselves become so bored that gossip becomes our creativity.

THE
MOONFLOWER
MONOLOGUES

If your loving is *love*, it can never be wasted.

THE
MOONFLOWER
MONOLOGUES

Seeeeeek.
Flourish.
Blooooooooom
(in the shadows of the moon).

It's noble (and kind) to acknowledge that
there will always be a story behind and
within the story—

Dimensions.

THE
MOONFLOWER
MONOLOGUES

Forgive your sweet self.

Fruit trees grow
where freedom flows.

THE
MOONFLOWER
MONOLOGUES

I knelt till I was empty—and here
I prayed for new wine.

And so the world lost its grip on me—

THE
MOONFLOWER
MONOLOGUES

Words from a true friend
are worth waiting for.

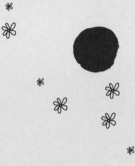

Moon milk, honeycomb,
violet silk, hearts at home,
swaying in the coral light,
music, candles,
burning bright—

Nights, sweet nights (with you).

THE
MOONFLOWER
MONOLOGUES

I turn my entire being toward the sun—
*I want to know what you are saying, in the
big, the small, & everything in between.*

THE
MOONFLOWER
MONOLOGUES

The female form—how she moves in the light of freedom, dancing the way she was created—breathtakingly rococo.

You'll know you've healed, when the catalyst that broke you, eventually gets your internal thank you—

THE MOONFLOWER

MONOLOGUES

Chives in the fruit bowl,
floral honey in the fridge,
sheets on the windows,
& lace curtains, lying unfitted
on every bed—

In between.

It's madness to think I'd ever be able to begin; my surroundings must be exceptional. I need candles and silence and spiced scents; wine & milk (together, stirred); hours ahead of me so the heavy layers of my day fade into the aromas of dinner; my bright-eyed babes, deep and pretty in sleep; his kiss, like fire (he must be away); hair twisted into a French eclair, while lavender soaks away storms. And if I could talk to the wind, I'd welcome her in.

I'll lie, I'll stand, I'll sit & sway—maybe I'll prune daisies between the turn of each page—

And everything after the beginning needs no ceremony, just time—

Books.

I'm learning purpose remains the same
even though expression can forever change.

Imagine, again.

THE MOONFLOWER
MONOLOGUES

In the nighttime places,
still her lungs breathe free;
in the darkest of spaces,
she has all that she needs.

In the midnight walking,
truth's voice was clear;
in the underground search,
not far—but near.

She lay down her swords,
her songs took their place;
she stood on the shores,
her heart in the chase.

Rest, sit back,
the seeds are sowing;
rest, sit back,
the heart is growing.

Her hands begged to help,
but they were told to lay;
while her feet were tired,
truth lengthened her day.

Gaining ground
the long way around,
the heart way,
the sure way,
a new way,
her new day—

Made whole.

* For Charlene

THE
MOONFLOWER
MONOLOGUES

A revolution sounds fanciful,
noble, reckless—cool-esque,
written within catchy love songs,
marching signs, and protests.

But a revolution takes courage,
traveling far beyond trends;
it starts in shadowed places,
and dares to turn bends.

A revolution is honest,
a walk the other way,
making changes,
not adhering,
not following common sway.

Ever just wake up & need fields?

THE
MOONFLOWER
MONOLOGUES

Sometimes it's heart work, to see the light again—other times, a simple good night's sleep!

Come with me,
I want to show you more,
away from all this noise.

I will be
awaiting overhead,
away from all the noise—

The secret place.

THE
MOONFLOWER
MONOLOGUES

Shrug off the unpleasantries and keep on loving!

When our hearts beat dim, cloaked in pain, we have the privilege of choice:

To stumble the long way round, tripping on the hazards of our own bitterness, or lean into the depths and bravely release bright love to come out cleansed—

Heal.

THE
MOONFLOWER
MONOLOGUES

Making the unnecessary a sidewalk and
the purposeful the straight and narrow—

Lady Wisdom.

❃

❃

❃

Everything you see in creation has been
made with a place and purpose; every
living thing, big or small, has intention.

❃

❃

❃

THE
MOONFLOWER
MONOLOGUES

Hearts on fire,
Yours in mine,
Velvet sweets,
Honeydew wine,

Lunar lips,
Purple eclipse,
Orange sands,
Flower-filled lands,

Hearts on fire,
Yours in mine,
Midnight dreams,
Summertime shine,

Blue-flamed love,
Daisies and doves,
Lilac sands,
Honey-filled lands.

Fools start fights.
Friends shed light.

Faith   makes   life   interesting.

It was an aroma
from the heart,
a simple breeze
forming a simple word,
and behind it,
possibilities,
new beginnings—
hope.

Just one word,
melting inner ice sculptures,
warming feet that had been cold for years,
lighting honey candles.

It was all there,
in just one word,
hidden in the breath of a sweet . . .

"Hello."

THE
MOONFLOWER
MONOLOGUES

The questions danced high
on the walls,
floors,
and ceilings,
rounding up and
bringing home
answers to feelings.

May my heart take the shape of the
bravest words I write.

I know it's been dark for the longest of whiles.

What you are learning can only be taught—
here. The truth you're finding can only be
revealed—here.

Be here.
Sow your tears   here.

And when the moonlight rises to full—

Bloom—here.

THE MOONFLOWER
MONOLOGUES

Toil,
turn soil,
search within,
without,
question
& search,
kneel,
sing,
pray—

You'll visit your depths, you'll mull
and cull, & you'll usually end up
where you left but with grit & gold,
a heart made bold.

And you'll name this time a gift.

Can we pen a poem together?
I asked.
Can we paint a song?
Can we dance by dawn light?

Art makes love and light last long—

Create together.

Fall asleep in love.

THE
MOONFLOWER
MONOLOGUES

Take words.
Weave looms—together
in bona fide shades.

Have gravity.
Involve magnitude—
in love, beyond time, in essence.

Arrive sometimes with flowers
& cake
& words,
and know when it's not time for cake—
and only whiskey will do.

Cultivate and tend to your gardens.
Water the soil where you can safely fall,
be you—

Friendship.

THE
MOONFLOWER
MONOLOGUES

There are some things you just
need to write on scrap paper
and tuck into your shoes.

THE
MOONFLOWER
MONOLOGUES

Lady, you be you, dance your gentle
sway & never underestimate the power
of—"Are you okay?"

THE
MOONFLOWER
MONOLOGUES

It looks so very pretty on you—

Tenderness.

THE
MOONFLOWER
MONOLOGUES

Expression is an exploration—
and discovering the purpose
of your soul: life's ultimate
treasure—

Dig.

179

Wash off the war,
let the tears fall—

Nightcap.

THE
MOONFLOWER
MONOLOGUES

There have been moments, real moments, when I thought the ocean ate the sun for breakfast, and it was lost, forever. It was here the words found me. They came to teach me a thing or two about me, about my Creator, about hope, about belonging, and about not. Like an invitation, the words begged me to write them in all kinds of places. And as the sun's mercy rose, again and again and again, dark night after dark night, their sounds began to change—as did I too.

I want you to be part of every part of my life.

THE
MOONFLOWER
MONOLOGUES

When you hear a story, sing this line back
to yourself: *There's more to this than I know—*

Mercy.

Sweet love, try not to despise your shadow walking—pretty things grow and shape here. And if you are standing on a mountain peak, drenched in the sun, light lanterns and drink floral milk—here.

MOONFLOWER

If you ever hear, "I'll make it work," fall effortlessly from the mouth of any, you are likely in the company of a magic kind of human.

Known for their unique élan to turn nothing into something—and something into anything. Blooming all year round, they are the kind that will take nuisance and make romance of it; they will help you see a missed deadline as a magic moment to trust the synchronicity of the Great Decider; and they will turn up on your birthday with a bag full of confetti, candles, and a heap of tangerine cellophane and suddenly—it's art. Canceled plans raise no qualm, because their kind find the dance (in everything)—even if it's resting on the threshing room floor, creating pillows from straw.

Their kind are found in all shapes and sizes, usually helping other life stories bloom. They take wrong turns and dare to see them as a chance to learn something new.

If you ever hear the noble words, "I'll make it work," you are likely in the company of this magic kind of human. Linger longer—

Improvisers.

I'm learning many things—bravery is showing up in places where fear lives and doing things anyway. I'm learning that assumptions are boring whether you are making them or minding them.

THE
MOONFLOWER
MONOLOGUES

When the front words are unable to express the backstory, sing!

Frustration—a gift.

Beginnings are waves carrying hearty expectations; many like to play in their breakers.

But only some bounce in the swells of the middle, where the rhythms of the undertow cause feet to surrender and hearts to float.

The billows of the middle lead to the shores of finish line festoons, and the middle of anything is pure bravery.

THE
MOONFLOWER
MONOLOGUES

Think about impossible things—often.

THE MOONFLOWER
MONOLOGUES

There are times in vibrant crowds
and lessons learned by night,
days of tears and heart work,
summers golden, glowing, bright—

Seasons.

Love sets us f r e e e e e e e
love is not a grip,
all of us—purposed vessels
along adventure's trip.

I made camp in your promises & waited
till the morning.

THE
MOONFLOWER
MONOLOGUES

Gratefulness can change—everything.

THE
MOONFLOWER
MONOLOGUES

How beautiful that a mere moment in
prayer expands to rivers of oil pouring
over and through our lives—

THE
MOONFLOWER
MONOLOGUES

Peace exists—open your arms.

My heart broke,
and it bled flowers.
I sang kindly
(within, without)
afraid bitterness would settle in:

All is well.
All is well.
All is well.

Then
the tears came
and didn't stop
for a while.
Then
I healed —

197

THE
MOONFLOWER
MONOLOGUES

There are seasons in my life when words
alone are dry and poesy is like a desert
trek in high heat—

only tears will do.

And I'm learning
not to hold them back.

THE
MOONFLOWER
MONOLOGUES

There she goes again,
taking water from my eyes.
Surely, if she sets the seas,
she guides my tears like tides—

The moon.

THE
MOONFLOWER
MONOLOGUES

People:
we mustn't contain them;
they come in,
and they go out.
It's okay.
Don't fret if space between you and another
stretches far.

It's okay.
People are vessels;
they carry things,
beautiful things.
And sometimes vessels need to voyage from
one land to another—
without you.
It's okay.
Space between is change, and change—
It's okay.
Breathe. Let go. Breathe. Let go.
Love will let you let them go.
Hold them with your heart,
but not your grip.
It's okay, sweet love, it's okay.

THE
MOONFLOWER
MONOLOGUES

Sometimes there are things you need
to do that won't make sense to anyone.

THE
MOONFLOWER
MONOLOGUES

Is your heart hungry for truth & flowers?
Eat such things for breakfast.

THE
MOONFLOWER
MONOLOGUES

You get to choose which voices you give
volume to.

THE
MOONFLOWER
MONOLOGUES

Summer brought the busy—not in the way one might imagine. I was busy—leaning into some heart work. Busy in the midst of a growing family, leaning into some heart work, busy. Healing amid long beach walks, longer nights, a mother's calling, and cups of tea. My heart—coming up for air, busy in prayer. I was busy in the stillness, allowing my busy heart to heal—and it took a busy lot of time.

THE
MOONFLOWER
MONOLOGUES

Improvisers lack nothing.

THE
MOONFLOWER
MONOLOGUES

Posture your heart—and let love move.

THE
MOONFLOWER
MONOLOGUES

Leave your decision-making far from the night;
the weeds always seem thicker there.
The promise of morning,
rising with flowers and feasts,
a full stomach and light,
can see even the roughest seas
calmed in just one bite.

The heaviness (from those dark, dark nights) began to feel forever away. So far that not even its echoes could wrap a cloak around me like they once did, convincing me I was better that way.

How kind not to notice that the darkness was being swallowed whole by the light.

I'm always curious about my own impulses when asked to jump into change unexpectedly. My fierce "yes!" woke all the reluctant parts in me. And I remember crying from the relief in the shower and asking God if it was okay that I felt this way. And I remember Him so clearly saying, "Yes!"

And so He placed me in the summer flowers—I never knew so many could exist at once.

It was a place to carelessly throw time into open spaces (for just a little while), where bread was eaten and broken with just a few, and my love for time alone wasn't questioned. And it held me so, in its flowers.

Kind sounds came from outside my window—my goodness, that magic, magic window. I remember imagining one just like it, moons ago. And in real time, from her glorious openness, I sat there, for hours some days, allowing life to remind me of forgotten things. There was a violin once—and another time, a full chorus line.

A box of free flowers was left on my doorstep one day with
a note that said, "Take me." And another day I accidentally
found a bottle of moonflowers on purpose.

I walked the unfamiliar streets over and over, and they felt
much like familiar little corners buried in my imagination.

I was *being*—in the beauty.
Resurrecting parts within,
parts that for a season I thought, *Better gone,*

And I felt God near,
nearer than I've ever known.
Seen, even.
His love notes, speaking to me.
Deeply personal miracles,
yet to be articulated, if ever.

Although many bear witness to your joy,
only few will know the deep battles you fight to keep it.

How kind not to notice that the darkness was being
swallowed whole by the light—until I did.

THE
MOONFLOWER
MONOLOGUES

New season, new he(art).

Blooming can look like many things. It can look like swimming in a sea of hearts. Quiet nights. Shifting priorities. Being alone—this too can be a kind of blooming. Gathered the in company of many—blooming. Sometimes it's waking up eager, early, & ready; other times, letting eyelids laze a little longer—slowly, blooming.

It can look like sitting on the living room floor with your kin, wasting time well. And sometimes it's a calendar full of bonanzas—bright, full, & bursting.

Blooming can be intimate or beautifully loud, standing on a summit, the secret place, or lying beneath starry clouds. Blooming can be internal, bright, deep, & true. . . .

And blooming can look different for me, for them, for you.

These milky soliloquies had some things to tell me, my heart was eager to listen, and as the sun's mercy rose again and again and again, dark night after dark night, their sounds began to change—as did I too.

This monologue, a gift to you. Her pages, truths after the storms.

She's a midnight igniter, nighttime revolutionary, moonlit encourager—a catalyst for growth.

I didn't know that she, too, would become a book, not at all, until suddenly—she was.

GRATITUDES

A glorious band of moonflowers chaperoned this vision with open hands (and hearts) to see these golden pages materialize. Thank you, you've given this book paper wings—I'll forever celebrate you:

Caleb Guinery, the love of my life and holder of dreams, your love for me and faith in God has awoken my eyes to the zillion miracles that happen simply every day—I love you; I love us. My little loves Peaches Wilde, Hopps Golden, and Junee Moon: my muses, because of you, life is beautiful! I love being your mumma.

A very big and special thank-you to Holly Masters, Tony Masters, Morgan Printing, Skie Peterson, Melissa Theilmann, Ryan Perno, and Kaylene Langford—without you, these pages would not exist. I could never conjure enough words or gestures to truly thank you for the love you have sown and poured into this creation (and me). I love you forever.

I want to take a special moment to honor all the behind-the-scenes hands & hearts that have worked in many different capacities on the early and ongoing processes of this book—enabling her pages to materialize from dream state to published form. Mum and Dad, Mumma and Pappa Guinery, Nedra Springer, Annette Kelsey, Sharee Gray, Bonnie Gray, Selene Sheerin, Teresa Archer, Amanda Jones, Sarah Quinn, Cassia and Garren Walton, Jenny Webb, Matt Webb, Lisa Byers, Ilsa Wynne-Hoelscher, Alex Carlyle, Dan and Hannah Gorry, and Rachael Valentine.

Thank you to Kevin Kotur and Andrews McMeel Publishing for welcoming me into your family of beautiful literature—I'm so grateful for your creativity and how you nurture the artist—thank you for taking these books into new spaces and faraway places (with such love and care).

Thank you to the plethora of generous family and friendships that surround my world (near and far) that have cheered me on, hemmed me in, met me in the eye of life's storms, packed books, offered advice, and clinked glasses with me when life has called for it—I feel blessed and humbled by you (you know who you are)—and I love you!

A massive thank-you to YOU (the reader), the original catalysts aka the Kickstarter backers who set these pages on their way. You have shown up (again & again) with your love, and it's overwhelmingly beautiful!

I wish I could make bouquets with the gold of my heart, because words alone are unable to express the fullness of my gratitude.

Sincere songs of gratitude to my Lord and Creator—what a privilege it is to be a vessel and create (because You first created me).

ABOUT THE AUTHOR

Tess Guinery is a dancer by upbringing, a designer by trade, and an artist by calling. After graduating from the Karl von Busse Institute of Design in Australia, she started her own freelance business, soon establishing herself as a sought-after creator with design work bursting at the seams. After seven fond years in the design industry, Tess intuitively pressed pause to take a sabbatical—its intention, to explore her inner artist. This purposeful time led to the making of her tangible art piece *The Apricot Memoirs*, whose bright and spirited pages touched audiences all around the world. Tess's latest collection, *The Moonflower Monologues*, calls readers deeper into the places they've feared to tread, while inspiring them to face the night seasons of the soul with boldness and courage. These days, Tess calls the wholesome town of Murwillumbah home along with her stuntman husband and their three spirited daughters. Her art is in the everyday.